Dear Reader,

Welcome to the *My Spin on Life Diary*. This is your place to write about anything that's on your mind or in your heart. If you can't think of something to write about, use the spinner to get a fresh idea!

Here's what to do:
- **Twirl the spinner arrow and let it land on a symbol.**
- **Open the book to see which two Diary Starters the symbol matches. Choose the starter you want to write about.**
- **Flip to the first open page and write about that subject. You may want to complete the sentence exactly, or the Diary Starter may get you thinking of another idea to write about. That's O.K., too.**

Write a paragraph or write two pages—it's up to you. The idea is to have fun filling your diary with your very own dreams, thoughts, memories, and experiences. It's all yours, so go to it!

Your friends at American Girl

Diary Starters

- If I could do today over, I would . . .
- Tomorrow would be an amazing day if this would happen:

- If my pet could talk, today he (or she) would say . . .
- If I could have any animal as a pet, it would be a _____, because . . .

- Wow! I just won an airline ticket to anywhere. I'm packing my bags for . . .
- The greatest place I've ever been was _____. Here's what made it so amazing:

- If I were in charge of the world . . .
- If I were named school principal for a day, my new rules would be . . .

- A superpower I could have used today is . . .
- If I could be invisible tomorrow, here's where I'd go:

- Today I really needed a _____. Here's why:
- If I'm ever in a jam, I'd want to talk to _____, because . . .

- Tonight I hope I dream about . . .
- If I were granted one wish, I would wish for . . .

- I'm dying to tell _____ the good news about . . .
- If I could pick up the phone and call anyone anywhere, I'd call _____ to find out . . .

- If I had a crystal ball, I'd want to know . . .
- If I could read anyone's mind, I'd choose . . .

- If a story about my day was in the newspaper, the headline would be . . .
- If I wrote an advice column, the advice I'd give myself today would be . . .

- If I were the lunch lady, tomorrow I'd serve . . .
- I had a _____ day at school because . . .

- If I could've been a fly today, I would've landed _____ so that I could find out . . .
- Here's something that really, really bugs me:

You can tell me anything.

And then what happened?

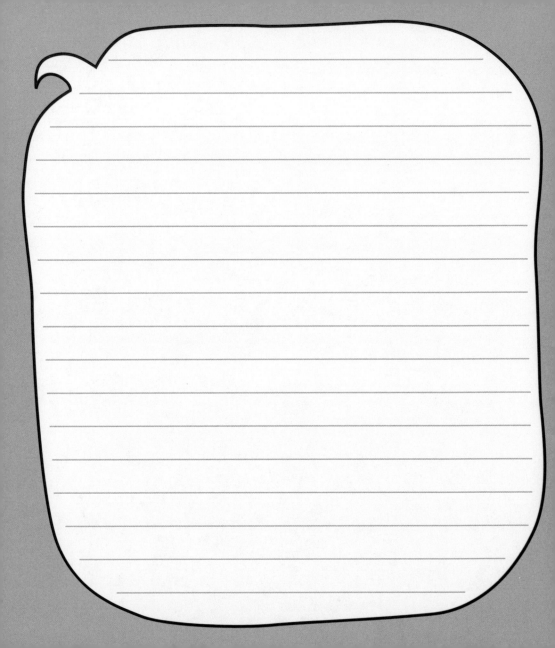

That's amazing.

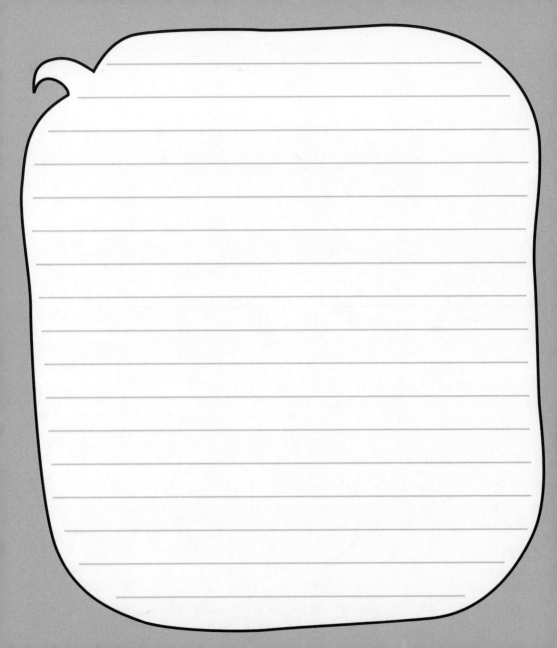

Tell me about it.

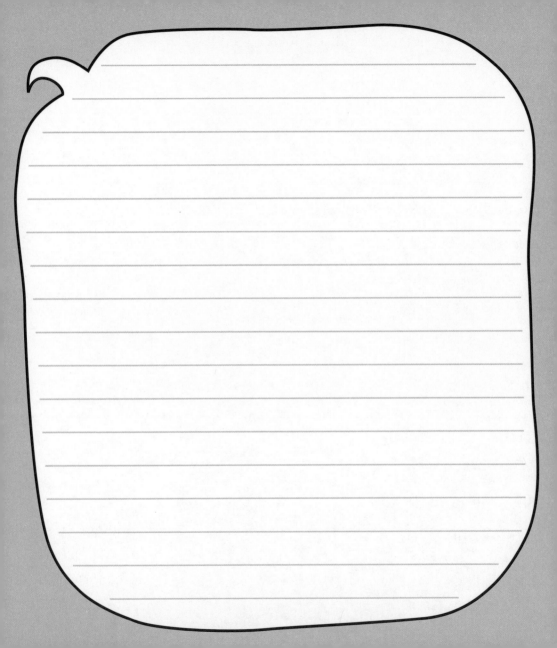

Keep talking!

You can tell me anything.

Tell it . . .
er, write it . . .
like it is!

I hear you!

Let it out.

Your secret's safe with me.

I'm listening!

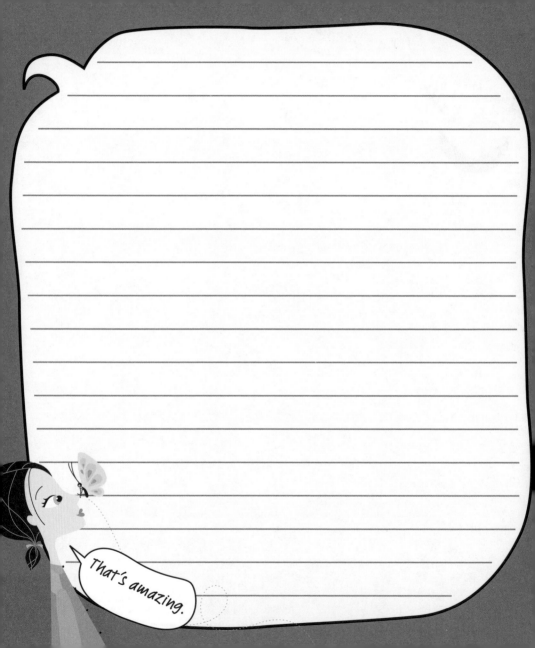

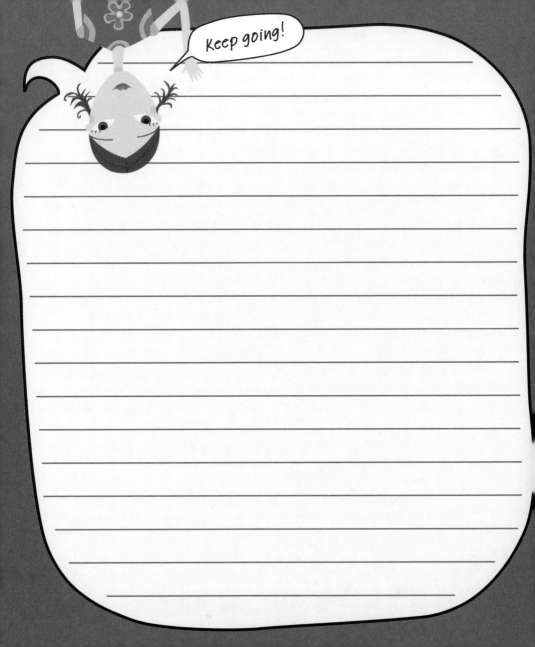

You can tell me anything.

That's amazing.

Now's your chance. Let it out.

Tell me about it.

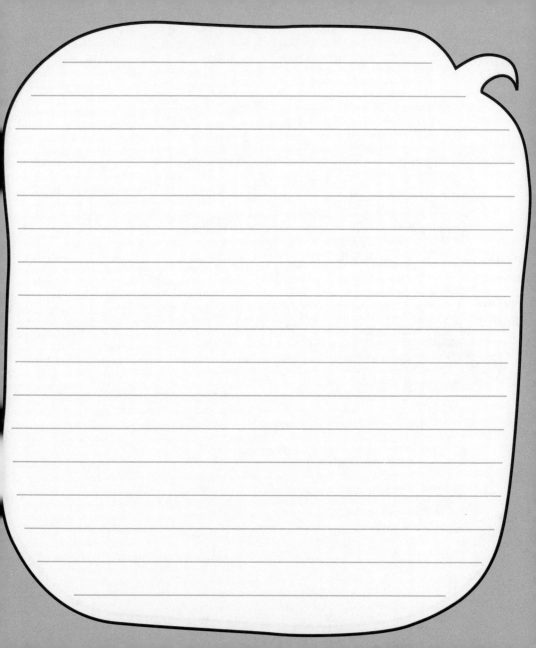

Tell me more!